(Traditional Tales)

Stories About Food

Retold by
Sharon Hurst

STAGE 1

www.kapadokyakitap.com

Kapadokya ELT.
Retold by Sharon HURST
Typesetting & Design Metin AYDOĞAN
Pictures drawn by RÜZGÂR
Cover by Ali İMREN
Operating pressure HTC Offset Printing in Ankara
ISBN: 978-975-9944-124-52-2

Anafartalar Mah. Kazım Karabekir Caddesi Öğün İş Hanı No: 40/60
06050 İskitler-ALTINDAĞ / ANKARA Tel. & Fax: (+90312) 312 72 57
Web: www.kapadokyakitap.com • E-mail: info@kapadokyakitap.com

Kapadokya Readers

Easy Starters
* The Easter Egg Hunt, Sharon Hurst
* The Last Biscuit, Sharon Hurst
* The Christmas Turkey Mystery, Sharon Hurst
* The Football Match, Sharon Hurst
* Carol and Tom's Wedding, Sharon Hurst
* Hannah's New Bedroom, Sharon Hurst
* Jack's Driving Test Adventure, Sharon Hurst
* Jack's Wisdom Tooth, Sharon Hurst
* Mothers' Day, Sharon Hurst
* A Trip to London, Sharon Hurst
* Bonfire Night, Sharon Hurst
* Hasan's Visit, Sharon Hurst

Stage 1
* The Phoenix Bird and Other Tales, R. A. Green
* Gulliver's Travels, Jonathan Swift
* Persuasion, Jane Austen
* Peter Pan, James Matthew Barrie
* The Mermaid and Other Tales, Hans C. Andersen
* Animal Stories, Sharon Hurst
* Vegetable Stories, Sharon Hurst
* Stories About Food, Sharon Hurst
* Sam's New School, Sharon Hurst
* The Jones Family, Sharon Hurst

Stage 2
* Alice in Wonderland, Lewis Carroll
* Anne of the Green Gables, L. M. Montgomery

Stage 2 (suite)
* Stories From Edgar Allan Poe, Edgar Allan Poe
* Moby Dick, Herman Melville
* The Children of New Forest, Captain F. Marryat
* The School Holidays, Sharon Hurst

Stage 3
* Tom Sawyer, Mark Twain
* Huckle Berry Finn, Mark Twain
* Uncle Tom's Cabin, Harriet Beecher Stowe
* The Call of The Wild, Jack London
* The Picture of Dorian Gray, Oscar Wilde

Stage 4
* Short Stories,
* David Copperfield, Charles Dickens
* Oliver Twist, Charles Dickens
* Treasure Island, Robert L. Stevenson
* Jane Eyre, Charlotte Brontë

Stage 5
* Little Women, Louisa May Alcott
* Pride and Prejudice, Jane Austen
* Wuthering Heights, Emily Brontë
* Silas Marner, George Eliot
* The Thirty Nine Steps, John Buchan

Stage 6
* A Tale of Two Cities, Charles Dickens
* A Song of Six Pence, Archibald Joseph Cronin
* The Mystery of the Woman in the Mirror, Teri Martini
* The Pearl, John Steinbeck
* Great Expectations, Charles Dickens

Level: 1

The Gingerbread Man

Part 1

Once upon a time there was a little old man and a little old woman. They lived together in a cottage in the countryside. There was a long winding path from the road to their house.

Nearby was a forest with lots of trees. The old couple liked to walk in the forest. There were also lots of farms nearby. Some of the farms grew wheat, others grew vegetables.

Not all the farmers grew crops, some kept animals. Some of the fields had cows, others had sheep. There were also chickens at some of the farms. Every morning the little old man and his wife heard the cockerels crowing.

Every morning after breakfast the old man sat in his favourite chair and he read the newspaper. The little old woman liked to cook. Sometimes she made cakes and sometimes she made biscuits.

One morning the little old man and the little old lady were eating their breakfast.

"What are you doing this morning?" the little old woman asked her husband.

"I think I will sit in my chair and read the newspaper," the little old man replied.

The little old man picked up the newspaper and sat in his favourite chair.

"What are you doing this morning?" the little old man asked his wife.

"I think I will do some baking," replied the little old woman.

The little old woman went to the cupboard and took out her cookery book. She turned over the pages and looked at the recipes.

"I can't decide what to bake today," she said to herself, "I made a fruit cake yesterday and a chocolate cake before that."

The little old lady looked at lots of recipes for biscuits and cakes.

"I know," said the little old lady, "I will bake some gingerbread biscuits."

The little old lady put 2 **tablespoons** of syrup into a pan. She added a tablespoon of treacle and a tablespoon of water. Then she put 1 teaspoon of ground cinnamon and 1 teaspoon of **ground** ginger into the pan. Finally the little old woman weighed 85 grams of soft brown sugar and put it in the pan.

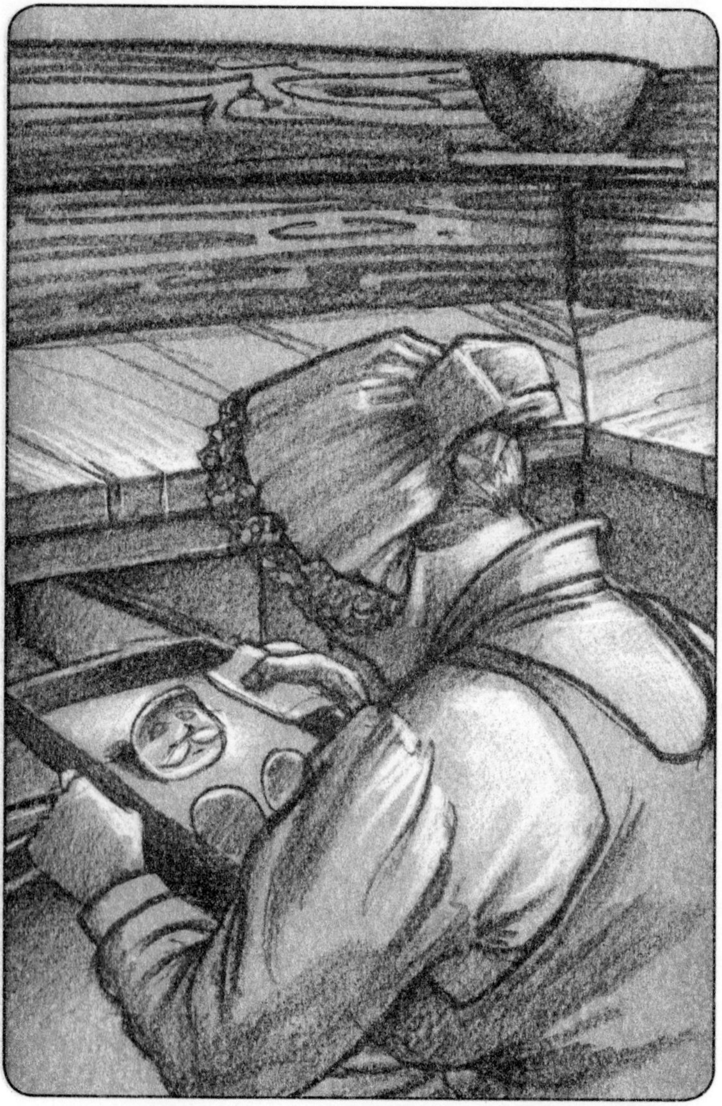

She heated the mixture in the pan and stirred it with a wooden spoon. The mixture soon boiled and the little old woman took the pan off the heat.

She cut 90 grams of margarine into small chunks and added it to the mixture. Then the little old woman added half a teaspoon of **bicarbonate of soda**. She weighed 225 grams of flour and added it to the mixture. She stirred it with her wooden spoon. The mixture was like dough now.

The little old lady put the dough in the fridge and made a cup of tea.

About half an hour later the little old lady put some flour on the table and put the dough on top. She took her rolling pin out of the drawer and rolled the dough. Soon the dough was flat and half a centimetre thick.

The little old lady cut out circles *(about 3-4 centimetres in diameter)* from the dough and put them on a baking tray.

There was some dough left over and the little old lady made the dough into a man. She gave him raisins for eyes and buttons.

The little old lady switched on the oven to 180 degrees and put the trays inside.

The biscuits took 10-15 minutes to cook.

Part 2

Suddenly the little old lady heard a voice in the oven.

"Let me out! Let me out!" shouted the voice.

The little old lady rushed to the oven and opened the door.

"**Oh my goodness**!" exclaimed the little old lady.

The gingerbread man jumped off the tray, he danced across the kitchen and ran out of the house.

The little old woman and the little old man ran to the door.

"Come back! Come back!" they shouted, "we want to eat you!"

But the gingerbread man ran down the path.

"Run, run as fast as you can, you can't catch me I'm the gingerbread man!" the gingerbread man sang back at the little old man and his wife.

The gingerbread man ran across a field. In the field was a cow.

"Stop, stop, little gingerbread man!" **mooed** the cow, "you look very tasty."

The cow started to chase the gingerbread man across the field. But the gingerbread man ran even faster.

"Run, run as fast as you can, you can't catch me I'm the gingerbread man!" the gingerbread man sang back at the cow.

The cow ran and ran but she could not catch the gingerbread man.

The gingerbread man ran across another field and passed a gate. Behind the gate was a horse.

"Stop, stop, little gingerbread man!" **neighed** the horse, "you look very delicious."

The horse reached across the gate. But the gingerbread man ran even faster.

"Run, run as fast as you can, you can't catch me I'm the gingerbread man!" the gingerbread man sang back at the horse.

The horse jumped over the gate and chased the gingerbread man. Behind the horse was the cow and behind the cow were the little old man and his wife.

The gingerbread man ran on and on. He ran very fast.

Eventually he met a sly old fox.

"Stop, stop, little gingerbread man!" called the fox, "I want to talk to you." But the fox was licking his lips.

The gingerbread man didn't want to talk he wanted to run.

The fox started to chase the gingerbread man across the field. But the gingerbread man ran even faster.

"Run, run as fast as you can, you can't catch me I'm the gingerbread man!" the gingerbread man sang back at the fox.

The fox ran quickly. He ran faster than the horse, the cow, the little old man and the little old woman. He followed the gingerbread man through a forest. The path led to a river.

The gingerbread man stopped at the river. He did not know what to do. Soon the cunning fox arrived.

"I'll help you," the fox offered, "jump on my tail and I will take you across the river. I will keep you dry."

The gingerbread man heard the horse's hooves and the cow's moos. In the distance he also heard the little old man and the little old woman.

So the gingerbread man jumped on the fox's tail. The fox began to swim across the river.

"My tail is hurting," complained the fox, "you are too heavy. Jump onto my back."

The gingerbread man jumped on to the fox's back.

Then the sly fox said, "my back is aching now, jump on to my nose."

The gingerbread man jumped on to the fox's nose.

Soon they reached the other side of the river. The cunning fox threw back his head and tossed the gingerbread man in to the air.

Then down fell the gingerbread man and snap went the fox's mouth.

And that was the end of the gingerbread man.

The End

COMPREHENSION QUESTIONS

Answer the following questions about the story.

1. Where did the little old man and woman live?
2. What crops grew on the nearby farms?
3. What animals lived on the farms?
4. What did the little old couple hear every morning?
5. What did the little old woman like to cook?
6. What did the little old man do after breakfast?
7. Which recipe did the little old woman choose?
8. What ingredients did she put in the pan?
9. The mixture boiled. What ingredients did she add next?
10. Where did the little old lady put the dough?
11. What shape were the biscuits?

12. What did the little old woman use for the gingerbread man's eyes?

13. How long did the biscuits take to cook?

14. What did the little old lady hear?

15. The little old lady opened the oven. What did the gingerbread man do?

16. What did the gingerbread man shout?

17. The gingerbread ran across a field. What was in the field?

18. Where was the horse?

19. What did the horse do?

20. What animal did the gingerbread man meet next?

21. How did the gingerbread man cross the river?

22. How did the fox cross the river?

23. The fox reached the other side of the river. Where was the gingerbread man now?

24. What did the fox do?

25. What happened next?

VOCABULARLY QUESTIONS

1. Write a sentence using each of the following words:

A) recipe

B) mixture

C) oven

D) sly

E) river

2. Some of the farms grew wheat. Name 5 other crops: *(use a dictionary)*

3. The old woman is cooking. List 5 verbs that describe her actions: *(use a dictionary)*

4. Look through the story and choose a word from the list to complete the sentences below:

complained shouted offered asked exclaimed

A) "What are you doing this morning?" the little old woman ________ her husband.

B) "Let me out! Let me out!" ________ the voice.

C) "Oh my goodness!" ________ the old woman.

D) "I'll help you," ________ the fox.

E) "My tail is hurting," ________ the fox.

5. Match the animal to the noise it makes: *(use a dictionary)*

bark neigh miaow crow moo

A) cockerel

B) horse

C) cow

D) dog

E) cat

GRAMMAR QUESTIONS

1. Change the following sentences into the future tense:

A) She heated the mixture in the pan.

B) The little old lady made the dough into a man.

C) The biscuits took 10 minutes to cook.

D) The horse jumped over the gate.

E) Soon the cunning fox arrived.

2. Make the following words plural:

A) biscuit

B) cake

C) teaspoon

D) lady

E) fox

3. Complete the following sentences using prepositions:

A) They lived together ________ a cottage.

B) The old man sat ________ his favourite chair.

C) She turned over the pages and looked ________ the recipes.

D) She put some flour ________ the table.

E) "Jump ________ my tail," said the fox.

WRITING PRACTICE

1. Re-write the story in your own words.
2. The little old man and little old lady did not catch the gingerbread man. Write about what happened to them during the chase.
3. The little old lady made the gingerbread biscuits. Re-write the details in the form of a recipe.

GLOSSARY

Part 1

once upon a time: a traditional beginning for stories.

tablespoon: equivalent to 15 millilitres.

ground: in the form of a fine powder.

bicarbonate of soda: raising agent also known as baking powder.

Part 2

oh my goodness: an expression of surprise.

moo: the noise a cow makes.

neigh: the noise a horse makes.

Level: 2

The Little Red Hen

Part 1

Once upon a time there was a little red hen. The little red hen lived on a farm in the countryside. She was a very pretty hen. She had silky feathers and black eyes. Her feathers were a rusty red colour and her beak was yellow.

The farm was quite old. Some of the gates were broken and some of the barns had holes in their roofs. But the animals were all happy.

There was also a pig, a mouse and a duck on the farm.

The farmer looked after his animals well. He did not keep them shut inside. He let them roam about the farm and wander in the fields.

In the spring the farmer was very busy. He prepared the fields and planted the crops. First he ploughed the fields.

Next the farmer planted the seeds. This year he wanted to grow some wheat. Before he planted the seeds he put several scarecrows in the field. Then he walked up and down the field sprinkling the seeds into the fresh soil.

The birds circled above the field, but the scarecrows frightened them and so they did not fly down and eat the seed.

In the spring there was lots of rain and sunshine and soon the seeds began to grow.

The summer was long and dry and the wheat grew tall and strong in the summer sun. Every day the farmer went to look at the wheat. He mended the fence around the field to stop the farm animals from walking in the field and trampling his lovely wheat.

At the end of the summer the farmer went to the fields to look at the wheat.

"A few more days and it will be ripe," he said.

So for the next few days he sharpened his tools and tidied up the barn.

Then he went back to the fields and looked at the wheat again.

"Today the wheat is perfect," he said.

The farmer spent the next few days cutting the wheat and gathering it all together to sell to the **miller**. The animals watched him from the farmyard. On the last day the farmer did not close the gate.

The little red hen decided to wander in the field. She found some wheat and picked it up in her beak. She carried it back to her friends in the farmyard.

"I am going to plant this wheat," the little red hen announced to her friends. "Does anyone want to help me?"

"Not I," said the pig.

"Not I," said the duck

"Not I," said the mouse.

The little hen was upset.

"Right, well, I will plant the wheat myself," the little red hen informed her friends.

So she wandered back out of the farmyard, through the gate and into the field.

She looked around the field and chose the sunniest spot. She loosened the earth with her beak and planted the seeds carefully. Then she covered the seeds with soil.

"I feel very pleased," the little red hen said to herself.

The little red hen went back to the farmyard. She flapped her wings and flew up to her favourite branch in the tree. From this branch she looked into the field.

The little red hen looked after the wheat and went everyday to watch it grow.

At last the wheat was golden. Its long tall stems swayed in the breeze. The little red hen knew it was ready to be cut.

Part 2

The next day the little red hen called her friends in the farmyard.

"My grains of wheat have sprouted and grown," she informed the other animals. "Who will help me to cut the wheat?" she asked.

"Not I," said the pig.

"Not I," said the duck

"Not I," said the mouse.

The little hen was upset.

"I see," said the little red hen dejectedly. "It doesn't matter I will cut the wheat myself."

The little red hen left the other animals in the farmyard and went into the barn. She picked up a little **scythe** in her beak and carried it to the field.

She carefully cut the stalks of wheat with the scythe. Then she dragged the stalks with her feet. Eventually she dragged the wheat all the way back to the farmyard.

The other animals were lying down in a corner of the yard. The little red hen walked over to her friends.

"Who will help me to take the wheat to the miller?" the little red hen asked her friends.

"Not I," said the pig.

"Not I," said the duck

"Not I," said the mouse.

The little hen was worried. She knew it would be hard work to take the wheat to the miller by herself.

So she searched in the farmyard for some string to tie the wheat together. Then she carried the wheat to the miller with the string in her beak.

"Good evening, Mr Miller," the little red hen greeted the miller. "I have grown some wheat. Will you grind it into flour?"

"You have come to the right place," replied the miller and he took the wheat from the little red hen. "Come back tomorrow and your flour will be ready."

The little red hen walked home happily and fluttered up into her tree.

The next morning she pecked around the farmyard for her breakfast. Eventually the other animals came to the farmyard to look for food.

"I am going to the miller to collect my flour today," the little red hen told the other animals, "will anyone help me to carry it?"

"Not I," said the pig.

"Not I," said the duck

"Not I," said the mouse.

The little red hen sighed loudly.

"Then I will carry it myself!" she said.

The little red hen walked to the windmill. She collected her bag of flour. It was heavy in her beak and she walked back very slowly.

At last she reached the farmyard. The sun was just setting. The little red hen put her bag of flour into the barn and quickly fell asleep.

The next day she dragged her bag of flour out of the barn.

"Please will someone help me to carry the flour to the baker?" she pleaded to the other animals.

"Not I," said the pig.

"Not I," said the duck

"Not I," said the mouse.

The little red hen was very disappointed in her friends.

"Then I will take it myself!" she said, but no-one was listening. The other animals were all looking around the farmyard for food.

The little red hen picked up the bag of flour in her beak and set off to the baker. Several times she stopped to rest. But she did not give up.

Finally she arrived at the baker's shop.

"Mr Baker, please will you make my flour into a delicious loaf of bread?" the little red hen asked the baker.

"Of course I will!" replied the baker, "I will make a lovely crusty loaf."

The little red hen waited outside. The baker added yeast, salt, sugar and water to the flour. He kneaded the dough and left it to rise in the warm sunshine.

The little red hen waited very patiently. The baker kneaded the bread again and then put it in the oven.

The smell of the bread drifted outside. The little red hen was very hungry. Her **tummy** began to **rumble**.

"Little red hen!" called the baker, "your bread is ready."

The baker put the bread into a paper bag.

"Thank you, it smells delicious," said the little red hen.

The little red hen carefully carried the bread back to the farmyard. The other animals very quickly came to see the bread.

The little red hen opened the bag and took the loaf out. It smelt delicious and the other animals stood by expectantly.

"**I don't suppose** anyone wants to help me to eat this bread, do they?" inquired the little red hen to her friends.

"I do," said the pig.

"I do," said the duck

"I do," said the mouse.

"Well you're not!" she said, "I am going to eat this fresh, crusty loaf all by myself!"

The other animals watched as the little red hen ate every crumb of her delicious loaf.

The End

COMPREHENSION[1] QUESTIONS

Answer the following questions about the story.

1. Where did the little red hen live?
2. What colours were her feathers and beak?
3. What was the farm like?
4. What other animals lived on the farm?
5. What job did the farmer do first in the spring?
6. What did the farmer put in the fields before he planted the seeds?
7. What was the weather like in the spring?
8. What did the farmer do to stop the animals walking on the wheat?
9. Who did the farmer sell the wheat to?
10. What did the little red hen do with the wheat she found?
11. Her friends did not want to help the little red hen to plant her wheat. How did the little red hen feel?

---

(1) This means "understanding".

12. Where did the little red hen plant her wheat?
13. From where did she watch the wheat grow?
14. What did she use to cut the wheat?
15. How did she get the wheat to the farmyard?
16. How did she take the wheat to the miller?
17. What did the little red hen collect from the miller the next day?
18. Where did she keep the flour that night?
19. Her friends did not want to help her to carry the flour to the baker. How did the little red hen feel?
20. What did she ask the baker to do?
21. What did the baker add to the flour?
22. How did he make the bread?
23. How did the little red hen take the bread back to the farm?
24. The little red hen arrived back at the farm. What did she do next?
25. Who ate the bread?

VOCABULARLY[(2)] QUESTIONS

1. Write a sentence using each of the following words:

A) silky B) hole C) earth

D) scarecrow E) windmill

2. A farmer, a miller and a baker appear in the story. Write a description of the following country jobs: *(use a dictionary)*

A) blacksmith B) fletcher C) thatcher

D) gamekeeper E) farmhand

3. Identify 5 emotions referred to in the story and give an alternative: *(use a dictionary)*

4. The hen's feathers were described as silky. Use the following touch words in a sentence:

A) rough B) soft C) fluffy

D) gritty E) slimy

---

(2) This means "words".

5. Give 2 alternatives for the following words:

A) to roam

B) to mend

C) to gather

D) to announce

E) to sway

GRAMMAR[3, 4] QUESTIONS

1. Change the following sentences into the present continuous tense:

A) First he ploughed the fields.

B) The birds circled above the field.

C) He sharpened his tools and tidied up the barn.

D) The little red hen dragged the wheat back to the barn.

E) The little red hen carried the bread back to the farmyard.

(3) "Alternative" means similar.

(4) This means "language structure".

2. Change the following adjectives into adverbs and use them in a sentence:

A) slow

B) careful

C) happy

D) dejected

E) loud

3. A noun has been underlined in each sentence below. Use an adjective to describe the noun:

A) The ________ farm was in the countryside.

B) The farmer put several ________ scarecrows into the field.

C) During the ________ summer the wheat grew tall.

D) The little red hen walked to the ________ windmill.

E) The baker put the ________ bread into the bag.

WRITING PRACTICE

1. Re-write the story in your own words.
2. You are the duck. Write the story as the duck, including reasons for not helping the little red hen.
3. Write about a journey you have made to the countryside.

GLOSSARY

Part 1

once upon a time: a traditional beginning for stories.

Scarecrow: made from rags in the form of a man to scare birds away.

miller: a person who grinds wheat into flour.

Part 2

scythe: a special tool with a round blade for cutting wheat and similar crops.

tummy rumbling: the noise of hunger in the stomach.

I don't suppose: indicates that a negative answer is expected.

Level: 3

The King Who Ate Too Much

Part 1

Once upon a time there was a young prince. The prince lived with his father, the king and his mother, the queen.

They lived in a land far, far away. Their home was a beautiful palace. The palace was made from the finest building materials. It had marble floors, **stained glass** windows and huge mosaics. Inside the palace there was a large reception room, a ballroom, a dining room, a throne room, 20 bedrooms and 20 bathrooms, and a huge kitchen.

All the rooms had the most expensive furniture from around the world. The chairs came from France, the sofas from Italy and the beds from Switzerland. The curtains were made from fabric spun with gold. The sheets on the beds came from Egypt. There were paintings on the walls by very famous artists.

The king and queen had only one child, the prince. After they married they waited a long time for a baby to arrive. Then the prince was born.

"A baby is born!" declared the royal announcer.

"A beautiful baby boy!" the queen said to the king.

"A son and heir!" the king said to the queen.

But the king and queen spoiled their son. They gave him everything. His nursery was full of every type of toy. In the palace were lots of servants. The young prince was quick to learn. The servants never refused the young prince anything.

"I want to go in the garden," the young prince told his **nanny**.

"Then we will go and play in the garden," his nanny replied.

"I want to go to the park," the young prince told the chauffeur.

"Then I will take you to the park," the chauffeur replied.

But the prince's favourite person was the cook. The young prince loved to eat. The young prince often went to the kitchen.

"I am hungry," the young prince complained, "I want a biscuit."

"I have just made your favourite chocolate cookies," the cook replied, "here, take two."

The young prince did not have many friends. He was often bored. He ate to pass the time. At first it was just snacks. Then he ate more and more at mealtimes.

When the prince was twelve years old he was quite **chubby**. He did not exercise very much and did not play sports. But the king and queen did not notice.

"Our little prince," remarked the queen one day, "he has such lovely chubby cheeks."

When the prince was eighteen years old he was really quite fat. He rarely went out of the palace. But still the king and queen did not notice.

"Our prince has grown into a strong young man," the king boasted one day.

When the prince was twenty-one years old the king died suddenly. The next day the prince was crowned the new king.

Before long he was eating more than ever. For breakfast he ate a large bowl of **porridge**. He liked a big spoonful of strawberry jam in the middle. Then he ate six eggs, four sausages, five **rashers** of **bacon**, fried tomatoes, mushrooms and eight slices of fried bread. But he was not full. He then ate seven slices of toast with butter and honey. He also drank several large cups of tea.

For lunch he ate a big bowl of soup. Tomato was his favourite but he also liked mushroom and chicken. Sometimes he ate all three. Then he ate four meat pies, a huge plateful of chips and six slices of bread. Then he ate three enormous slices of fruit pie, covered in **custard**. His favourite was apple pie but he also liked cherry pie. He also drank several large glasses of lemonade.

At four o'clock every day the king wanted afternoon tea. He ate lots of little sandwiches and even more cakes. He adored chocolate cake. The king often ate a whole chocolate cake.

In the evenings he ate a huge roast dinner. He like roast beef best, with roast potatoes, roast carrots and parsnips. He often ate nine **Yorkshire puddings**. Afterwards he liked several desserts. His favourite was meringue but he also liked jam sponge and sticky toffee pudding. He drank several large glasses of beer with his dinner.

The cook was very busy. Every day the king got bigger and bigger and every day his appetite grew as well.

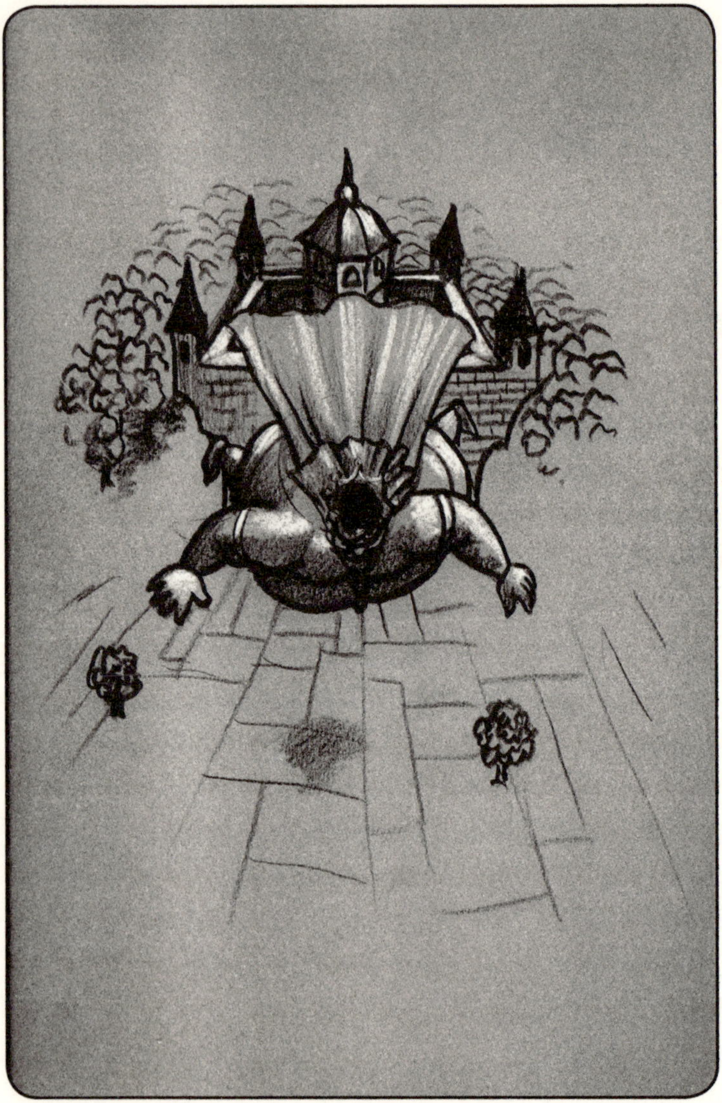

Part 2

After a few years the king did not go out. He did not sit in his throne room and meet his **subjects**. He did not ask about his country.

"When is my food ready?" was the only question the king asked.

All the king's wealth was gradually spent on food. The cook was very worried.

"How will I feed the king when the **treasury** is empty?" the cook asked everyone.

Then one day the king ate his enormous lunch as usual. Puddings were his favourite and on this day he not only ate a second portion, but a third, fourth and even a fifth.

"I am very full," the king said, "that meal was delicious."

But then the king started to feel very strange. Although he was fatter than ever he started to feel very light.

"I feel very strange," the king remarked to one of the servants.

The servant did not reply. He watched something very strange. The king started to float into the air. The king was very, very fat and he looked like a giant balloon.

Up, up into the air the king floated. He floated out of the dining room and out of the large front door.

"Oh, my goodness!" shouted the king, "where am I going?"

The king floated over his garden and down the long driveway. He floated across the road and over a farm. He looked down at the farm and saw the farmer's children. They were dressed in dirty rags. He saw some very thin cows in a field. He saw the farmer dragging a plough by hand.

"How can my neighbours be so poor?" the king wondered.

He floated on until he reached a small village. He saw the people dressed in rags. Everyone was very thin. Everyone looked very sad. The buildings needed repairs, windows were broken and roofs had holes in them.

"The people of this village must be very lazy," thought the king, "they do not look after themselves or their property."

The king floated on over mountains and across rivers. He floated over a forest. Men were cutting down the trees to use for firewood.

Then the wind blew the king high into the sky and across the land very quickly. Then the wind stopped and he gently floated down over a large city.

The king saw children sat in the street. They were begging for food. They were dirty and dressed in rags. The city was very quiet. The king was surprised. He saw a few men pushing a cart with rotten fruit and vegetables.

"Who will eat such food?" wondered the king, "and who will pay money for it?"

Everywhere the king went he saw poverty. People were starving, they had no money and their houses needed repairs.

Suddenly the king felt very ashamed. He was also very shocked.

"I have been very selfish. I have neglected my royal duty as king. My duty is to look after my people. But all I cared about was food," the king said sadly.

The wind took him back towards the palace and gently placed him down in the palace garden.

"Where have you been?" the servants asked. "We were worried about you."

"Prepare a royal feast!" declared the king. "Every subject is to come to the palace to eat!"

The king sent out a proclamation to every village, town and city in the kingdom.

The next day all the citizens came to the palace and ate all day long. The king ate nothing because he was so ashamed.

Then the king gave every subject a purse with 5 gold coins inside. The subjects were all happy and smiling and the children played games.

From that day the king toured his county every month. He gave money to the poor and sweets to the children. The people were not thin anymore and the king ate less and less. Finally the king was not fat anymore.

The End

COMPREHENSION QUESTIONS

Answer the following questions about the story.

1. Who did the prince live with?
2. Where did they live?
3. Where did their chairs come from?
4. Who was the young prince's favourite person?
5. What did the prince look like when he was 12 years old?
6. Which sports did he play?
7. What did the prince look like when he was 18 years old?
8. What happened when the prince was 21 years old?
9. What did the new king eat for breakfast?
10. What did the new king eat for lunch?
11. What happened at 4 o'clock every afternoon?

12. What did the new king eat in the evenings?
13. Why was the king's treasury becoming empty?
14. The king ate five portions of pudding one day. How did he feel?
15. The king floated over a farm. What did he see?
16. The king floated over a small village. What did the see?
17. Did the king think the people were hard-working?
18. The king floated over a city. What did he see?
19. How did the king feel?
20. What was the king's duty?
21. The king floated back to the palace. What did he tell the servants?
22. What did the king eat at the banquet?
23. What did the king give every citizen?
24. Afterwards what did the king do every month?
25. Did the king always eat too much?

VOCABULARLY QUESTIONS

1. Write a sentence using each of the following words:

A) nursery

B) chauffeur

C) chubby

D) wealth

E) rags

2. Fat and chubby are used in the story to describe the king. List 5 other words used to describe a person's size or stature: ***(use a dictionary)***

3. The furniture in the palace came from France, Italy and Switzerland. Name 5 other countries in Europe: ***(use a dictionary)***

4. The king lived in a palace. Describe in a sentence the other types of houses below: ***(use a dictionary)***

A) detached house

B) cottage

C) terraced house

D) bungalow

E) mansion

5. Give 2 alternatives for the following words: ***(use a dictionary)***

A) to notice

B) gradually

C) portion

D) selfish

E) duty

GRAMMAR QUESTIONS

1. Change the following sentences into the past tense:

A) The prince is playing in the nursery with his toys.

B) The king and queen will spoil their only son.

C) The cook is making a snack for the prince.

D) The prince is eating too much.

E) The king feels very ashamed.

2. Choose a joining word from the list below and use it in the sentences underneath:

- *so* *then* *but* *because* *and*

A) The king and queen are spoiling the prince ________ he is their only son.

B) The young prince ate too much ________ he did not play sport.

C) The young prince was becoming fat ________ his mother and father did not notice.

D) The young prince was hungry ________ he asked the cook for a biscuit.

E) The new king held a banquet ________ he gave everyone a purse with five gold coins.

3. Replace the object underlined in the sentences below with a suitable object pronoun:

- *him you me them us her it*

A) The king married the queen.

B) The cook saw the prince in the kitchen.

C) The king floated above his subjects.

D) The king did not sit on his throne.

E) The king gave some sweets to the children.

WRITING PRACTICE

1. Re-write the story in your own words.

2. You are a poor farmer. You live near the palace. Write about your life and how you feel about the king.

3. Write about how the king found a wife.

GLOSSARY

Part 1

once upon a time: a traditional beginning for stories that are not in a real setting.

stained glass: is coloured glass made into pictures.

nanny: a woman employed to look after children in their home. A 'snack' is food eaten between meals.

chubby: plump, or fat in a polite way.

porridge: made from oats and warm milk.

rasher: a slice of bacon.

bacon: thinly sliced pork meat.

custard: a sweet sauce made from milk and egg yolk.

yorkshire pudding: a made from milk, eggs and flour.

Part 2

subjects: The people ruled by a king are his subjects.
treasury: where a country's wealth is kept.